D1109280

AMERICAN HISTORY BY DECADE

The
1930s

Don Nardo

**KIDHAVEN
PRESS™**

THOMSON
GALE

San Diego • Detroit • New York • San Francisco • Cleveland
New Haven, Conn. • Waterville, Maine • London • Munich

© 2004 by KidHaven Press. KidHaven Press is an imprint of The Gale Group, Inc., a division of Thomson Learning, Inc.

KidHaven™ and Thomson Learning™ are trademarks used herein under license.

For more information, contact
KidHaven Press
27500 Drake Rd.
Farmington Hills, MI 48331-3535
Or you can visit our Internet site at http://www.gale.com

ALL RIGHTS RESERVED.
No part of this work covered by the copyright hereon may be reproduced or used in any form or by any means—graphic, electronic, or mechanical, including photocopying, recording, taping, Web distribution or information storage retrieval systems—without the written permission of the publisher.

LIBRARY OF CONGRESS CATALOGING-IN-PUBLICATION DATA

Nardo, Don, 1947–
    1930s / by Don Nardo.
      p. cm. — (American history by decade)
Summary: Discusses the political, economic, and cultural life of the United States in the troubled 1930s, focusing on the depression, the Golden Age of movies, and the threat of world war.
Includes bibliographical references and index.
  ISBN 0-7377-1515-4 (alk. paper)
1. Nineteen thirties—Juvenile literature. 2. United States—History—1933-1945—Juvenile literature. 3. United States—History—1919-1933—Juvenile literature. 4. United States—Economic conditions—1918-1945—Juvenile literature. 5. Depressions—1929—United States—Juvenile literature. 6. Popular culture—United States—History—20th century—Juvenile literature. [1. Nineteen thirties. 2. United States—History—1919-1933. 3. United States—History—1933-1945. 4. Motion pictures.] I. Title. II. Series.
  E806.N268 2004
  973.917—dc21
                              23.76
                                                                2002155397

Printed in the United States of America

3 9082 09274 5325

Contents

Strength of Character in the Face of Upheaval

The 1930s was one of the most **turbulent**, or active and disordered, decades in the history of the United States. American society underwent a number of sudden and major changes that altered the lives of millions of people, often for the worse. Many Americans suffered during the Great Depression, for example. This financial crisis caused large numbers of people to lose their jobs, so poverty increased. Because money was worth less and harder to come by, crimes also increased. There was a rash of bank robberies and gangsters had crime rings in several large cities.

Natural disasters also took a big toll on society. In the Midwest, generations of unwise farming methods and a period of very dry weather caused the soil to turn to dust. Much of the soil blew away, destroying the lives of many farming families. Thousands of them **migrated** to other parts of the country and tried to start new lives.

To deal with these problems, the federal government and other authorities decided to make some major changes. To help fight the terrible poverty created by the depression, the government created millions of new jobs. Some of these jobs helped to reverse the devastation done to the land. The government paid large numbers of people to teach farmers how to conserve good soil, plant new forests, and build dams. Meanwhile, federal and local police greatly expanded their efforts to fight crime.

One thing that did not change in the 1930s was the American character. Americans had long had a tradition of being hardworking and of finding ways to cope with hardship. Now, with the economy worse than ever, millions of families tightened their belts, pinched their pennies, and took whatever work they could get. Many did backbreaking, thankless jobs,

A farmer and his sons seek shelter from an Oklahoma dust storm in 1936. Severe storms ruined many Midwest farmers in the 1930s.

Children stack boxes of cranberries. Many people in the 1930s, including children, were forced to do backbreaking work.

like digging ditches, with little complaint. In addition, people actively searched for ways to relieve their feelings of worry and gloom. They went to the movies in record numbers and played games of all kinds on a scale that had never been seen before. Therefore, the 1930s was not only a decade of social upheaval, it was also a period in which Americans proved to the world, and to themselves, that they had unusual strength of character.

CHAPTER ONE

History's Worst Financial Disaster

One huge, shattering event dominated the world during most of the decade of the 1930s. This was the Great Depression. A **depression** is a period in which the economy of a country suffers a serious decline. Typically, many companies go out of business or have trouble making ends meet, and this causes large numbers of people to lose their jobs. That is what happened during the Great Depression, which began in 1929. It turned out to be the worst financial crisis in history. It caused much poverty and misery around the world for more than a decade.

Panic in the Stock Market

The economic downturn that led to the Great Depression was caused by the crash of the American stock market. On October 21, 1929, the prices of many **stocks** on the New York Stock Exchange suddenly dropped sharply. This caused thousands of people who owned these stocks to panic. They sold the stocks, taking huge losses. The fear this created made the stock prices drop even lower, prompting still more people to dump their stocks. In the days that followed, the situation spiraled out of control. And by the end of October the market's losses were an incredible $50 billion, the worst in its history.

Panic strikes Wall Street during the stock market crash of 1929. The crash set off the Great Depression of the 1930s, when millions lost their jobs.

This frightening stock market crash had a ripple effect on society as a whole. Many rich people whose fortunes had been built in the stock market lost everything and became almost penniless. Millions of ordinary people were also affected. Hundreds of banks closed and many of their customers lost their entire life savings. Also, the value of money had suddenly decreased. That meant that a person could buy much less for a dollar than he or she could before the crash. Out of fear, therefore, most Americans bought only what they needed to stay alive. This, in turn, caused stores to lose business. They had to lay off many workers and cut back on ordering new products from factories. As the ripple effect continued, many of those factories had no choice but to shut down or lay off many of their workers.

These layoffs caused the unemployment rate to skyrocket. It had been a fairly low 3 percent before October 1929 but rose to 9 percent by early 1930. In the next two years the jobless rate continued to rise and in 1932 reached 25 percent. That means that one out of every four American homes had no regular income to live on and had to borrow or beg for money just to put food on the table.

Meanwhile, the awful ripple effect of falling prices and growing poverty spread past America's borders. European countries had long depended on borrowing money from the United States, based on the long-standing strength of the American dollar. But now the dollar was worth much less.

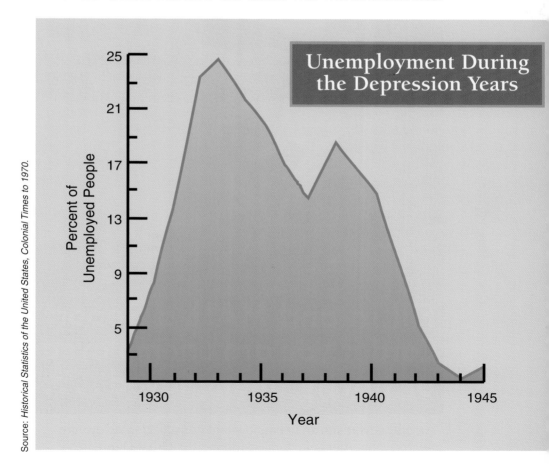

Source: Historical Statistics of the United States, Colonial Times to 1970.

Unemployment During the Depression Years

Percent of Unemployed People

Year

A poster advertises an unemployment census. Unemployment affected most American families during the Great Depression.

So the volume of trade between Europe and North America shrank and soon factories and stores across Europe had to lay off workers. Many other nations across the world suffered similarly from the economic upheaval in America.

Memories of Tough Times

The serious nature of that economic upheaval is best illustrated by the memories of people who endured the tough times of the 1930s. In Youngstown, Ohio, a man told the mayor, "After working at the steel mill for twenty-five years, I have lost my job, and I'm too old to get other work. If you can't do something for me, I'm going to kill myself."[1] In East Harlem, New York, a man who lived in an apartment building wrote to his congressman, saying, "It is now seven

Unable to find work, these men feel hopeless. Most workers spent months looking for any kind of paying job.

months I am out of work. . . . I have four children who are in need of clothes and food. . . . My rent is [over]due two months and I am afraid of being put out [thrown out]."[2]

Many cities had to resort to handing out bread to people to keep them from starving to death. Songwriter Yip Harburg, who lived in New York City, recalled that the bread lines "went for blocks and blocks around the park. The prevailing greeting at that time, on every block you passed, by some poor guy coming up, was: 'Can you spare a dime?'"[3] Harburg was so moved that he turned that phrase into a song. It became popular far and wide and many people saw it as the unofficial anthem of the Great Depression. Among its sad words were these:

Unemployed men wait in a bread line in New York. Private charities supplied food and other necessities to the needy.

Then and Now

	1930	2000
U.S. population:	123,188,575	281,421,906
Life expectancy:	Female: 61.1 Male: 58.1	Female: 79.5 Male: 74.1
Average annual salary:	$1,368	$35,305
Unemployment rate:	8.7%	5%

Source: Kingwood College Library.

They used to tell me I was building a dream with
   peace and glory ahead.
Why should I be standing in line just waiting for
   bread?
Say, don't you remember, they called me Al; it was Al
   all the time.
Say, don't you remember I'm your Pal! Buddy, can
   you spare a dime?[4]

A New Deal for the Country

Unfortunately, few Americans could spare even a dime to
help fellow citizens in dire need. Many people hoped the
federal government would help the homeless and hungry
and pull the country out of its economic slump. At first,
though, the government did little. President Herbert Hoover,
who served from 1929–1933, did not believe in what he
called "government charity." He said it would only make

President Herbert Hoover believed that private charities and local relief efforts should help the needy until the economy turned around.

people lazy and dependent on the government. Instead, private charities and state and local relief efforts would have to do the job.

Hoover's approach failed, however, as local charities and relief efforts were quickly swamped by waves of needy people. In contrast, Hoover's successor, Franklin D. Roosevelt, believed that the federal government had to play a major role in fighting the depression. He thought that the country needed a "new deal" from its leaders. So the programs he enacted came to be called the New Deal. In his inaugural address, delivered on March 4, 1933, he said it was time for a change of attitude. Both the government and people must face and conquer the fear that had gripped the country. "The only thing we have to fear is fear itself," the new president declared. "I shall . . . wage a war against the emergency as . . . if we were in fact invaded by a foreign foe."[5]

Roosevelt delivered on this promise. He pushed **bill** after bill through the Congress, each of which provided jobs or loans or other financial relief for the stricken country. He reopened most of the banks that had earlier closed. He also put almost 3 million Americans to work planting trees, building dams, and fighting forest fires. One of his most important achievements was the Social Security Act, passed in August 1935. It provided (and still provides) money to citizens

President Roosevelt initiated the New Deal, a plan to lift the country out of the Great Depression.

in need because of increasing age, unemployment, or sickness. Roosevelt also created the Tennessee Valley Authority (TVA). This was one of the most ambitious construction projects in world history. It built fifteen huge dams in the Tennessee River Valley, giving millions of Americans cheap electricity and providing years of work for tens of thousands of people.

The End of the Depression

Not all of Roosevelt's programs were as successful as these. So the country's financial recovery was slow and unsteady. But he kept the New Deal in place after he won the elections of 1936 and 1940. There is no doubt that the New Deal helped many Americans get back on their feet or at least survive. However, the biggest factor in ending the depression was the entry of the United States into World War II in 1941. When the country started producing enormous amounts of

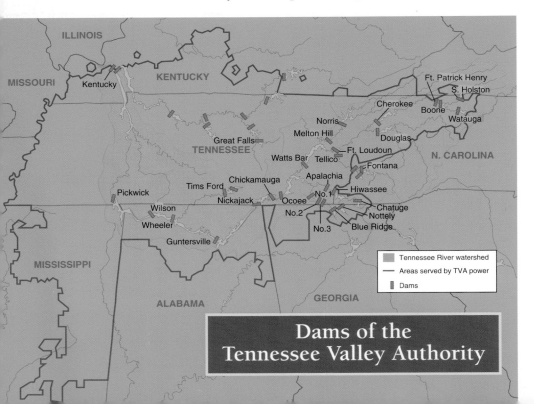

Dams of the Tennessee Valley Authority

A woman works in a defense factory during World War II. The
need for defense workers created many new job opportunities
for women.

ships, airplanes, guns, and food to wage the war, the economy steadily improved. Yet the memories of the worst financial disaster in history remained strong. Americans who
lived through the Great Depression never forgot the hard
times the country experienced in the uncertain decade of
the 1930s.

CHAPTER TWO

The Movies Raise People's Spirits

Tens of millions of Americans were out of work, struggling, fearful, or miserable during the economic upheavals of the 1930s. The need to laugh and escape the world's harsh realities became important to many people.

By far the most common way people tried to escape the gloom was to go to the movies. The motion picture had already been around for about three decades when the depression began. And movies had long been a popular pastime. But during the depression of the 1930s the need for escapist entertainment became bigger than ever before. Throughout the decade an estimated 80 to 90 million Americans went to the movies at least once a week. That was more than 60 percent of the country's entire population.

It might seem strange that so many people with so little money in their pockets would attend the movies so often. One reason was that movie tickets were relatively cheap. Most neighborhood theaters charged ten cents for adults and five cents for children in the early 1930s. By the end of the decade prices were not all that much higher—an average of thirty cents for adults and fifteen cents for children. Moreover, most theaters offered two movies, a cartoon, and a short newsreel for the price of admission. Most people felt that, for the money, it was the best entertainment deal around.

Demand for "Talkies"

Another factor that drew people to the movies in record numbers was the recent addition of sound to film. Until the late 1920s, movies had been silent. Inventors had experimented with sound since the turn of the century. But they had long found it difficult to **synchronize** the sound, that is, to make the spoken words match the movements of the actors' lips. Also, adding sound to a film was very expensive. And most studios were reluctant to spend the extra money.

All that changed, however, after the Warner Brothers Studio released *The Jazz Singer,* starring Al Jolson, in 1927. Much

Children wait in line outside a movie theater. The addition of sound to film increased the popularity of movies.

of the film remained silent. But the musical numbers had sound, as did a few scenes with spoken dialogue. When Jolson said, "Wait a minute; wait a minute. You ain't heard nothing yet,"[6] audiences cheered. After that the public demanded to see "talkies" and every studio rushed to install sound equipment. By 1930 nearly all films had sound, which helped keep moviegoers flocking to the theaters on a weekly basis.

The Jazz Singer was the first movie to include sound. Audiences loved the film's musical numbers and spoken dialogue.

King Kong was one of the most popular movies of the 1930s. Moviegoers enjoyed films that took their minds off their problems.

Into a World of Make-Believe

The tastes of these frequent moviegoers were reflected in the kinds of films that were popular in the 1930s. In general, people did not want to watch stories that were too realistic and reminded them of their personal troubles. Instead, they wanted to be swept away into a world of make-believe. In particular, they liked and demanded lighthearted entertainment, including musicals.

At first, most of the musical films were "reviews." In a review, singers, dancers, comics, and other stage and night-club entertainers put on their acts one after another. The filmed musical reviews had little or no plot to tie the various acts together.

The first movie musical to use music and dance to tell an actual story was *Forty-Second Street* (1933). The plot revolves around the personal lives of the director and stars of a Broadway musical. But the main musical number is much more complex and spectacular than anything that could be done on stage. The studios saw that this sort of spectacle sold a lot of movie tickets. So they kept on making musicals with big production numbers.

Much of the credit for the big production numbers of the 1930s goes to Busby Berkeley, a Broadway dance director hired by Warner Brothers in 1930. He developed a dance style that became very popular. It consisted of dozens and often hundreds of dancers dressed in flashy costumes and assembled on giant sets. As the performers danced in unison, the camera viewed them from all angles, even at floor level or from directly above.

The Hollywood Western Comes of Age

Another kind of film in demand in the 1930s was the Hollywood western. In the first half of the decade most westerns had very low budgets, so their quality was generally low. But the heroes, who were often singing cowboys such as Gene Autry and Tex Ritter, were very popular with moviegoers. Even the great western star John Wayne was forced into this mold in one of his early films. His daughter Aissa recalled: "My father could not sing at all, nor play the guitar. . . . [So] two men would stand off-camera, one singing, one strumming—my father faked it."[7]

In the second half of the decade, sound westerns began to come of age. Films like *The Texas Rangers* (1936) and *Wells*

Singing cowboy Gene Autry starred in many popular Hollywood westerns during the 1930s.

Fargo (1937) had bigger budgets and were more spectacular. The most popular and acclaimed of all the westerns of the 1930s was director John Ford's *Stagecoach* (1939). Audiences liked John Wayne as the Ringo Kid, a lonely gunslinger with a troubled past. And that character became a model for later movie western heroes.

Stagecoach was the most popular western movie of the 1930s.

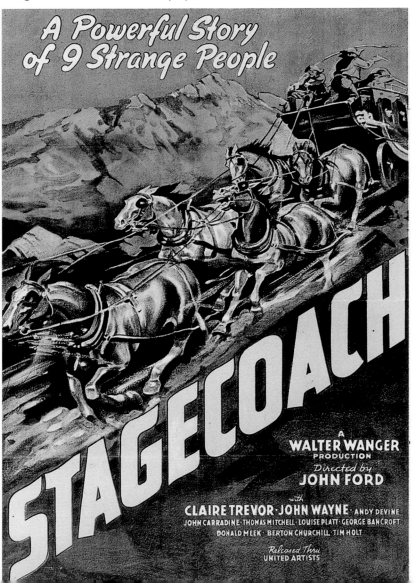

A Powerful Story of 9 Strange People

STAGECOACH

A WALTER WANGER PRODUCTION

Directed by JOHN FORD

with CLAIRE TREVOR · JOHN WAYNE · ANDY DEVINE
JOHN CARRADINE · THOMAS MITCHELL · LOUISE PLATT · GEORGE BANCROFT
DONALD MEEK · BERTON CHURCHILL · TIM HOLT

Released Thru UNITED ARTISTS

Gone With the Wind was the most successful movie of the 1930s. Americans easily identified with Scarlett O'Hara's troubles.

Gangsters, Monsters, and Colorful Costumes

Musicals and westerns were not the only kinds of films in demand among depression-era moviegoers. They also packed theaters to see gangster films like *Little Caesar* (1930); horror flicks like *Frankenstein* (1931); silly comedies like *Bringing Up Baby* (1938); and cartoons like Walt Disney's *Snow White and the Seven Dwarfs* (1937), the first full-length animated film.

In addition, moviegoers flocked to see "costume epics" such as *The Adventures of Robin Hood* (1938) and *Gone With the Wind* (1939). In fact, *Gone With the Wind,* about the American Civil War, was the most successful movie of the decade. Part of the appeal was the plight of the main character, Scarlett O'Hara. She lost everything in the war and had to start over from scratch, with only her wits and courage to guide her. This closely mirrored the experiences of many Americans in the 1930s. Scarlett's famous last line, "Tomorrow is another day," was a fitting message of hope to end a decade during which some people had believed all hope was lost.

CHAPTER THREE

Popular Leisure Activities of the 1930s

Although going to the movies was the single most popular leisure pastime in the 1930s, people turned to all manner of other forms of entertainment as well. Some of these activities had no other reward but enjoyment. Listening to the radio was one. In addition to music and news, there were weekly and sometimes nightly comedies and dramas. Mysteries such as *Sherlock Holmes* and *The Shadow* were particularly popular. And young people loved to listen to the adventures of the colorful crime fighter Dick Tracy. The most popular radio show of the decade was *Amos 'n Andy,* a nightly comedy about a black big-city cab driver (Amos) and his amusing friend (Andy). Some 40 million Americans—one-third of the nation—tuned in each night.

Other leisure activities combined entertainment with the chance of making money. This is not surprising. The Great Depression was in full swing and many people were willing to try almost anything to make some extra cash. Pinball machines were introduced in the early 1930s, for example. They became widely popular and people bet varying sums of money on the outcomes of the games. **Dance marathons** and bingo games also lured in crowds hoping to have fun and strike it rich at the same time.

The Last Left Standing Wins

Dance marathons were also called "Dance Derbies." In these public contests, young adult couples competed to see who

Millions of Americans tuned in to radio shows every night. *Amos 'n Andy* was the most popular radio show of the 1930s.

A marathon dancer collapses in her partner's arms. Marathon dance contests were popular in the 1930s.

could keep dancing the longest without falling either down or asleep. In some versions one partner was allowed to fall asleep as long as the other could hold him or her up and keeping dancing. Usually, the dancers were allowed to rest for fifteen minutes or less each hour. But the dancing went on twenty-four hours a day, seven days a week. Sometimes a live band provided the music, while other times an emcee played a phonograph. Most of the dances were slow. But once or twice each hour came a song with a faster beat. Over time, one by one the couples quit from sheer exhaustion, until one couple was the last left standing. The record was twenty-two weeks, three-and-a-half days.

Prizes for the winners of these dance contests were often as high as one thousand dollars. Sometimes the jackpot reached five thousand dollars. This was a lot of money in depression-era America. So it is not surprising that many young men and women entered dance marathons. Also, they often drew big crowds eager to find out which couple had the stamina to outlast the others. Sometimes the promoters who put on the marathons cheated to draw bigger crowds. A common tactic was to hire people to pretend they were contestants. These couples picked fake but seriously realistic-looking fights with one another. The brawls resembled those in modern professional wrestling matches and many people saw them as more entertaining than the dancing.

The darker side of the dance marathons was that the contestants risked their health. They got little or no sleep and could not eat regular meals. So some became ill, as well as exhausted, and two people even died. For these reasons, most states eventually outlawed the marathons. The ups and downs of these strange but compelling contests are the subject of the 1969 film *They Shoot Horses, Don't They?* starring Jane Fonda.

The Biggest Bingo Game on Record

Another game that attracted adults hoping to have fun and make a quick profit was Bingo, which is still played today. It is a very old game, a version called Keno being popular in the early 1800s. In the early twentieth century various forms of the game were played across America, having names such as Beano, Lucky, and Fortune. Many of these versions used hand-labeled cardboard for the game cards and dried beans for tokens.

The version that swept the country in the 1930s started with a New York toy salesman named Edwin Lowe. He enjoyed playing Beano and introduced it to his friends. One day one of them won a game and was so excited that, without thinking, she yelled "B-B-Bingo!" The name stuck and

Men and women play Bingo in Las Vegas. The game was very popular in the 1930s, drawing millions of players.

Lowe marketed it. He demanded that anyone running a public game and calling it Bingo pay him a dollar.

Lowe also expanded the game into its more familiar modern form. He hired a math professor to come up with more number combinations for the cards, making it more difficult to win. He also manufactured millions of printed game cards and wooden tokens. This version of the game reached its height of popularity in the 1930s, drawing large crowds. The biggest on record was in 1934 in Teaneck, New Jersey, where sixty thousand people played Bingo at the same time. Lowe eventually sold his Bingo game to the Milton Bradley Company for $26 million.

The Thrill of Phony Money

Another game with tokens swept the nation in the 1930s, one extremely popular with both adults and children— Monopoly. One reason for Monopoly's widespread appeal was that it involved winning money. Even though the money used in the game was phony, it gave depression-era players the illusion of getting rich quick.

A good deal of controversy surrounds the origins of Monopoly. The traditional tale is that it was invented by Charles Darrow, a salesman and inventor from Germantown, Pennsylvania. According to this story, after the 1929 stock market crash he pieced the game together, making little houses and tokens out of wood. He introduced the game to his friends. And they liked it so much they wanted copies of their own. So Darrow made several more copies of the game by hand and sold them for four dollars each. Eventually, Parker Brothers, a leading manufacturer of games, bought the rights to Monopoly.

Today, this story is disputed. Evidence suggests that Darrow copied the game from some earlier, similar versions. One was called "The Landlord's Game," another "Finance."

The thrill of winning large sums of play money and property made Monopoly the most popular board game of the 1930s.

Whoever the real inventor may have been, there is no doubt that Darrow and Parker Brothers made a fortune. In 1935 the company was producing twenty thousand copies of Monopoly a week. It was by far the best-selling game in America in the 1930s. People sometimes played for weeks at a time, always thrilled to pass "Go" and collect the two hundred dollars even if they could not actually spend it.

CHAPTER FOUR

World War Looms on the Horizon

The ravages of the Great Depression showed that the economies and fates of all nations were closely linked. Yet in a very real sense, the United States tried to shut out the rest of the world during the 1930s. Most Americans had come to think of Europe as distant and corrupt. In this view, the United States was democratic, modern, and forward-looking, while most European countries were old-fashioned and out of touch with American values. Americans also saw many Europeans as dishonest for not repaying loans the United States had given them in the past. Furthermore, the Europeans seemed always to be attacking and fighting wars with one another. By contrast, Americans saw themselves as a peaceful people who fought only when directly provoked.

For these reasons, during the 1930s the U.S. government sought to keep the country **isolated**, or separated from, the affairs and troubles of other nations. In May 1937 Congress passed the Neutrality Act. It was meant to keep the country **neutral**, or uncommitted to either side, in a European war. The act forbade Americans from giving loans to any foreign nations that were at war. It also stopped Americans from traveling on ships sailing from such nations.

This and other policies made most Americans feel like they were safe from getting involved in foreign wars. But it eventually became clear to many that this was an illusion. Throughout the decade the world became more and more dangerous. A major war finally did break out in Europe, and Americans found themselves divided about whether to get involved.

Americans Debate the War in Spain

Among the first signs that the United States could not and should not remain isolated was the Spanish Civil War. Spain was a republic, with a democratic form of government. But in 1936 the country's **Fascists**, those who wanted a dicta-

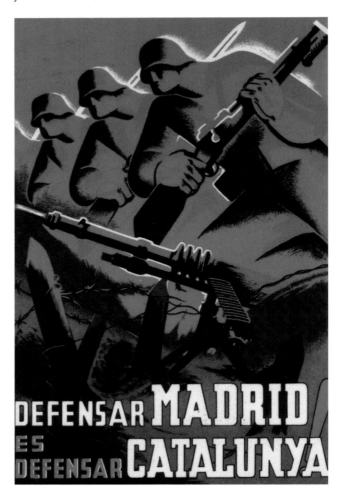

A poster from the Spanish Civil War illustrates armed soldiers, barbed wire, and says "Defending Madrid is Defending Catalonia."

Ernest Hemingway (second from right) meets with a journalist during the Spanish Civil War. He used his experiences in Spain to write a novel about the war.

tor to run the country, launched a revolution. Italy and Germany, which already had Fascist dictators, sent supplies, weapons, and troops to help the rebels.

American opinions about the civil war in Spain were sharply divided. Some people believed that the United States should take a stand for democracy and support the Spanish republicans. Others insisted that the country should stay out of the conflict. Officially the United States did remain neutral. However, a number of concerned Americans sent medical and other supplies to aid the republican cause.

In addition, a few Americans actually traveled to Spain and fought against fascism. Among them was the famous American novelist Ernest Hemingway. He later wrote about the war, which the Fascists won, in his book *For Whom the Bell Tolls*. Hemingway made the point that the conflict was like a warning bell for freedom-loving people everywhere. They must not sit back idly and allow the Fascists to take over the world.

An Independent Destiny for America?

In 1937 another important event made many Americans question the isolationist view. Japan, which had become very warlike in recent years, invaded large parts of China. Some Americans living in China were killed. And the Japanese sank a U.S. ship that was moving along a Chinese river.

President Roosevelt saw this event as a sign that sooner or later the United States would probably be drawn into a major war. He warned his fellow Americans that it had become "impossible for any nation completely to isolate itself from the economic and political upheaval in the rest of the world." Americans were "determined to keep out of war," he said, "yet we cannot insure ourselves against the disastrous effects of war."[8] Roosevelt wanted to make sure that the country could defend itself if it had to. So in 1938 he called for several new warships to be built.

Opposition to Roosevelt's position was still strong across America, however. Some people called the president a "warmonger." Many isolationists eventually banded together to form the America First organization. Stating its goals, the famous airplane pilot Charles Lindbergh said, "We believe in an independent destiny for America. Such a destiny . . . mean[s] that the future of America will not be tied to these eternal wars in Europe. . . . American boys will not be sent across the ocean to die."[9]

Roosevelt's Warning

The debate in America about getting involved in foreign wars got hotter than ever when Nazi Germany attacked Poland in September 1939. That event marked the beginning of World War II in Europe. Britain and France, the chief allies of the United States, declared war on Germany and its own ally, Italy. Yet America still remained neutral. President Roosevelt told the American people, "I hope the United States will keep out of this war. I believe that it will. And . . . every effort of your government will be directed toward that end." [10]

For the moment, neutrality seemed the best course for the United States. Roosevelt was still trying hard to address the economic problems of the Great Depression. That effort required all the money and other resources the government could muster. He did not want to involve the country in an expensive and draining war unless it was attacked.

Yet in the president's view, such an attack was likely to happen sooner or later. There seemed little doubt that the Fascists wanted eventually to dominate not just Europe, but

Polish women and children gather on a Warsaw street during the German invasion of Poland.

U.S. soldiers stand at attention in London during World War II. At the beginning of the war, few Americans wanted the United States to get involved.

the world. And these warlike countries would not hesitate to strike out at the United States when they felt the time was right. In an earlier speech, Roosevelt had warned what might happen if Americans ignored the mounting violence overseas. "Let no one imagine that America will escape," he said, "that it may expect mercy, that this Western Hemisphere will not be attacked." [11]

For the moment, however, most Americans did not pay heed to this warning. As the turbulent decade of the 1930s came to a close, few realized what was in store for the nation. True to Roosevelt's words, it would soon become part of the terrible world war presently looming on the horizon. That conflict would end up changing America and its place in the world in ways that no one in 1939 could possibly foresee.

Notes

Chapter One: History's Worst Financial Disaster

1. Joseph L. Heffernan, "The Hungry City: A Mayor's Experience With Unemployment," in William Dudley, ed., *The Great Depression: Opposing Viewpoints.* San Diego: Greenhaven Press, 1994, pp. 34–35.
2. Quoted in Howard Zinn, *A People's History of the United States.* New York: HarperCollins, 1980, p. 379.
3. Quoted in Studs Terkel, *Hard Times: An Oral History of the Great Depression.* New York: Random House, 1970, p. 20.
4. "Brother, Can You Spare a Dime?" (1932), words by E.Y. Harburg, music by Jay Gorney. Quoted in Diane Ravitch, ed., *The American Reader: Words That Moved a Nation.* New York: HarperCollins, 1990, p. 270.
5. Franklin D. Roosevelt, "First Inaugural Address," in Richard Hofstadter, ed., *Great Issues in American History: A Documentary Record, Volume II, 1864–1957.* New York: Vintage Books, 1960, pp. 355–357.

Chapter Two: The Movies Raise People's Spirits

6. Quoted in Ephraim Katz, *The Film Encyclopedia.* New York: HarperCollins, 1994, p. 1271.
7. Quoted in Aissa Wayne, *John Wayne, My Father.* New York: Random House, 1991, pp. 65–66.

Chapter Four: World War Looms on the Horizon

8. Quoted in Hofstadter, ed., *Great Issues in American History*, 1960, pp. 389–391.
9. Quoted in Wayne S. Cole, *Charles A. Lindbergh and the Battle Against American Interventionism in World War II.* New York: Harcourt, Brace, Jovanovich, 1974, pp. 87–88.

10. Quoted in Richard Hofstadter et al., *The United States: The History of a Republic.* Englewood, NJ: Prentice-Hall, 1976, p. 686.
11. Quoted in Hofstadter, *Great Issues in American History,* p. 389.

Glossary

bill: An act debated, passed, or voted down by Congress or another legislature.

dance marathons: Contests held during the 1920s and 1930s in which couples competed to see who could keep dancing the longest.

depression: A period in which the economy of a country suffers a serious decline.

Fascist: A member of a political group that advocates rule by a dictator.

isolated: Separate from others. A group or country that is against getting involved with foreign nations is said to be isolationist.

migrate: To travel, along with one's belongings, to another place to live.

neutral: A position in which a person, group, or country refuses to take sides in a dispute.

stocks: Shares in a company. Each share has a value that goes up when the company is doing well and down when the company is not doing well. If someone buys stocks for one dollar each and sells them when they are worth two dollars each, he or she makes a profit. If the value of the stocks goes down to fifty cents and the person sells, he or she takes a loss.

synchronize: To match up the voices in a movie with the visual images of the actors talking. When the sounds and visuals match, they are said to be "in sync."

turbulent: Very active, disordered, or unpredictable.

For Further Exploration

Books

Ralph Anspach, *The Billion Dollar Monopoly Swindle*. Published privately by Ralph Anspach, 1998. Contains a detailed account of the controversy surrounding who really invented the famous board game Monopoly. A bit challenging for grade-school readers but it reads like a fascinating detective story and is worth the effort.

Nancy M. Davies, *The Stock Market Crash of Nineteen Twenty Nine*. Parsippany, NJ: Silver Burdett Press, 1994. Explains the workings of the stock market and looks at the big crash that caused the Great Depression.

Don Nardo, *Franklin D. Roosevelt: U.S. President*. New York: Chelsea House, 1996. An easy-to-read volume that summarizes the life, struggles, and incredible accomplishments of one of the nation's greatest leaders, including his response to the Great Depression crisis.

David Parkinson, *The Young Oxford Book of the Movies*. New York: Oxford University Press, 1997. An excellent introduction to the art of filmmaking for young readers. Contains much about film history, including the advent of the sound era.

Gail Stewart, *The New Deal*. Parsippany, NJ: Silver Burdett Press, 1993. This well-written description of the New Deal of the 1930s is highly recommended.

Websites

Encyclopedia.com (www.encyclopedia.com). Links to an overview of the background causes and outbreak of World War II, with several links to related topics.

Library of Congress American Memory (http://memory. loc.gov). Displays several links to archives of many excellent photos taken during the 1930s. Look for "America from the Great Depression to World War II" especially.

StreetSwing.com (www.streetswing.com). Links to the dance marathons of the 1930s, including a list of some of the major ones and several sources for further research.

Yahoo!GeoCities (www.geocities.com). An excellent history of Hollywood in the 1930s and of the films of that era. Highly recommended.

Index

REDFORD TWP. PUBLIC LIBRARY

Picture Credits

Cover Photo © Hulton|Archive by Getty Images

© The Advertising Archive Ltd., 20

© Arthur Rothstein/CORBIS, 30

© Bettmann/CORBIS, 17, 28, 32

© CinemaPhoto/CORBIS, 23

Chris Jouan, 13

© Hulton|Archive by Getty Images, 21, 34, 35, 37, 38

Library of Congress, 11, 14, 15

Library of Congress, Prints & Photographs Division,
    FSA-OWI Collection, 5, 6, 12, 22

National Archives, 8

Photofest, 24, 25, 27

© Swim Ink/CORBIS, 10

About the Author

Historian and award-winning author Don Nardo has written many books for young people about American history, including *The American Revolution, The Mexican-American War, The Declaration of Independence,* and biographies of Presidents Thomas Jefferson, Andrew Johnson, and Franklin D. Roosevelt. Mr. Nardo lives with his wife Christine in Massachusetts.